S0-ABD-663

SUPER SIMPLE DIY

MAKE A DINOSAUR

YOUR WAY!

Elsie Olson

Consulting Editor, Diane Craig,
M.A./Reading Specialist

COOK MEMORIAL LIBRARY DISTRICT
413 N. MILWAUKEE AVE.
LIBERTYVILLE, ILLINOIS 60048

Super Sandcastle

An Imprint of Abdo Publishing
abdobooks.com

ROARR!

abdobooks.com

Published by Abdo Publishing, a division of ABDO, PO Box 398166, Minneapolis, Minnesota 55439. Copyright © 2019 by Abdo Consulting Group, Inc. International copyrights reserved in all countries. No part of this book may be reproduced in any form without written permission from the publisher. Super SandCastle™ is a trademark and logo of Abdo Publishing.

Printed in the United States of America, North Mankato, Minnesota
102018
012019

 THIS BOOK CONTAINS RECYCLED MATERIALS

Design: Sarah DeYoung, Mighty Media, Inc.
Production: Mighty Media, Inc.
Editor: Megan Borgert-Spaniol
Content Consultant: Benjamin J. Garner
Cover Photographs: iStockphoto; Shutterstock
Interior Photographs: iStockphoto; Shutterstock

The following manufacturers/names appearing in this book are trademarks: Crayola®, Elmer's®, POOF®, Scotch®, SOLO®

Library of Congress Control Number: 2018948780

Publisher's Cataloging-in-Publication Data
Names: Olson, Elsie, author.
Title: Make a dinosaur your way! / by Elsie Olson.
Description: Minneapolis, Minnesota : Abdo Publishing, 2019 | Series: Super simple DIY
Identifiers: ISBN 9781532117169 (lib. bdg.) | ISBN 9781532170027 (ebook)
Subjects: LCSH: Dinosaurs--Juvenile literature. | Handicraft--Juvenile literature. |
    Creative activities and seat work--Juvenile literature.
Classification: DDC 680--dc23

Super SandCastle™ books are created by a team of professional educators, reading specialists, and content developers around five essential components—phonemic awareness, phonics, vocabulary, text comprehension, and fluency—to assist young readers as they develop reading skills and strategies and increase their general knowledge. All books are written, reviewed, and leveled for guided reading and early reading intervention programs for use in shared, guided, and independent reading and writing activities to support a balanced approach to literacy instruction.

TO ADULT HELPERS

The projects in this book are fun and simple. There are just a few things to remember to keep kids safe. Some projects may use sharp or hot objects. Also, kids may be using messy supplies. Make sure they protect their clothes and work surfaces. Be ready to offer guidance during brainstorming and assist when necessary.

CONTENTS

BECOME A MAKER

A makerspace is like a laboratory. It's a place where ideas are formed and problems are solved. Kids like you create amazing things in makerspaces. Many makerspaces are in schools and libraries. But they can also be in kitchens, bedrooms, and backyards. Anywhere can be a makerspace when you use imagination, inspiration, **collaboration**, and problem-solving!

IMAGINATION

This takes you to new places and lets you experience new things. Anything is possible with imagination!

INSPIRATION

This is the spark that gives you an idea. Inspiration can come from almost anywhere!

MAKERSPACE TOOLBOX

COLLABORATION

Makers work together. They ask questions and get ideas from everyone around them. **Collaboration** solves problems that seem impossible.

PROBLEM-SOLVING

Things often don't go as planned when you're creating. But that's part of the fun! Find creative **solutions** to any problem that comes up. These will make your project even better.

IMAGINE A DINO

DISCOVER AND EXPLORE

Dinosaurs lived millions of years ago. But you can see them in books, on TV, and in movies. You can learn all about them in museums and on the internet. What is your favorite kind of dinosaur? What do you like about it?

GET INSPIRED!
See page 24

IMAGINE

If you could make any dinosaur, what would it be like? Would it look like a real dinosaur that lived long ago? Or would it look completely different? Would it be as big as a car? Or as small as a penny? Remember, there are no rules! Let your imagination run wild!

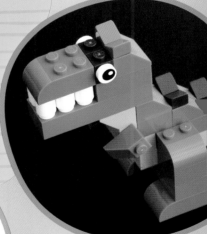

BRING YOUR DINO TO LIFE

It's time to turn your dream dinosaur into a makerspace marvel! What did you like most about your dino? Was it the big teeth? The spiky tail? The shiny scales? How could you use the materials around you to create these features? Where would you begin?

INSPIRATION

Dinosaurs Alive! is part of an Ohio theme park. It has more than 50 life-sized robotic dinosaurs! The park's builders worked with **paleontologists** to create the dinosaurs. Each model is based on a type of dinosaur that actually lived!

COLLABORATE!
See page 28

BE SAFE, BE RESPECTFUL

MAKERSPACE ETIQUETTE

THERE ARE JUST A FEW RULES TO FOLLOW WHEN YOU ARE BUILDING YOUR DINO:

1. **ASK FOR PERMISSION AND ASK FOR HELP.** Make sure an adult says it's OK to make your dino. Get help when using sharp tools, such as scissors, or hot tools, like a glue gun.

2. **BE NICE.** Share supplies and space with other makers.

3. **THINK IT THROUGH.** Don't give up when things don't work out exactly right. Instead, think about the problem you are having. What are some ways to solve it?

4. **CLEAN UP.** Put materials away when you are finished working. Find a safe space to store unfinished projects until next time.

GATHER YOUR MATERIALS

STRUCTURE

These are the main materials you will use to build your dinosaur's body.

Every makerspace has different supplies. Gather the materials that will help you build the dinosaur of your dreams!

CONNECTING

These are the materials you will use to hold your dinosaur together.

DECORATIONS & DETAILS

These are the materials you will use to make your dinosaur look cool and bring it to life!

COLLABORATE!
See page 28

⚠ STUCK?

LOOK BEYOND THE USUAL CRAFT SUPPLIES! THE PERFECT SHAPE MIGHT BE IN YOUR KITCHEN CABINET, GARAGE, OR TOY CHEST. SEARCH FOR MATERIALS THAT MIGHT SEEM SURPRISING.

BUILD YOUR DINO'S BODY

Every structure is made up
of different shapes. How can
you put shapes together to
make your dream dino?

GET INSPIRED!
See page 24

⚠ STUCK?

TRY MAKING YOUR DINO SMALLER OR BIGGER! YOU COULD USE A PAIR OF DICE INSTEAD OF A CARDBOARD BOX, OR A SOCCER BALL INSTEAD OF A MARBLE.

INSPIRATION

A *T. rex* can be broken down into ovals, rectangles, and triangles. What everyday items have these shapes?

WHAT WILL YOUR DINO DO?

What do you want your dinosaur to do? Knowing this will help you figure out what materials you could use to construct your dino.

Will it stand on a shelf? Then you need sturdy legs to support the body!

Wide, flat feet will help support your dino's weight.

IMAGINE

WHAT IF YOUR DINO LIVED UNDERWATER? OR ON MARS? HOW WOULD THAT CHANGE YOUR DINO?

PROBLEM-SOLVE!
See page 26

Will it hang?

Then you need to use lightweight materials.

Your dino's weight will need to be balanced for it to hang evenly.

15

Paleontologist Jack Horner was an advisor for the famous dinosaur movie series *Jurassic Park*. In 2009, he began working with other scientists to create a live mini dinosaur. He planned to use **DNA** from dinosaurs' modern relatives, chickens!

Will it float?
Then you need to use **buoyant** and **waterproof** materials!

16

COLLABORATE!
See page 28

Will it breathe fire? Then you need a mouth that's large enough and sturdy enough to attach flames to.

Look for materials that give off or reflect light to look like fire.

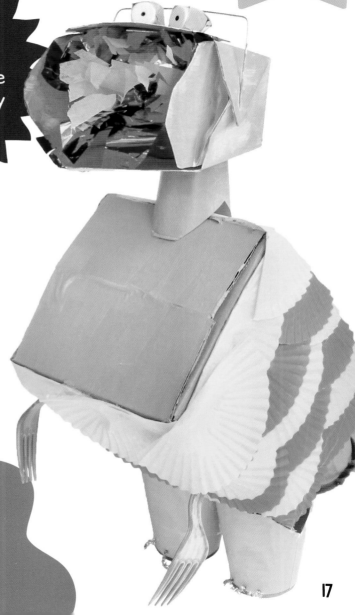

⚠ STUCK?

YOU CAN ALWAYS CHANGE YOUR MIND IN A MAKERSPACE. ARE YOUR FLAMES NOT LOOKING RIGHT? COULD YOU MAKE THEM INTO WINGS INSTEAD?

CONNECT YOUR DINO

Will your dinosaur be **permanent**? Or will you take it apart when you are finished? Knowing this will help you decide what materials to use.

TOTALLY **TEMPORARY**

PAPER CLIPS STUCK IN SOFT MATERIALS

POSTER PUTTY

BRASS FASTENERS

THUMBTACKS

PROBLEM—SOLVE!
See page 26

IMAGINE

WHAT IF YOUR DINOSAUR HAD TO BE TAKEN APART AND RECYCLED INTO A NEW DINO? WHAT WOULD YOUR NEW SHAPE LOOK LIKE?

A LITTLE STICKY

DOUBLE-SIDED TAPE

STICK-ON VELCRO

SUPER STICKY

DUCT TAPE

HOT GLUE

DECORATE YOUR DINO

MARBLES

BREATH MINTS

COTTON SWABS

Decorating is the final step in making your dinosaur. It's where you add **details** to your dino. How do your decorations bring your dino to life?

GET INSPIRED!
See page 24

PLASTIC SPOONS

FEATHERS

DUCT TAPE

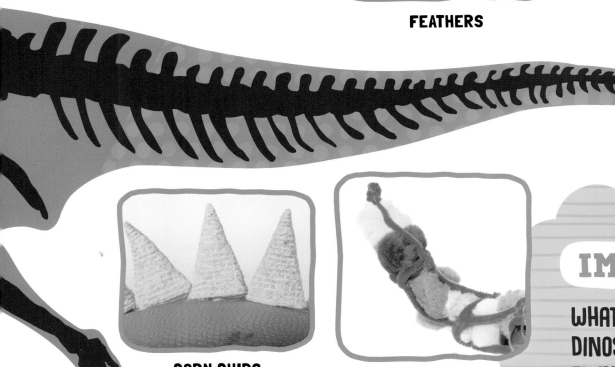

CORN CHIPS

**CHENILLE STEMS
AND POM-POMS**

IMAGINE

WHAT WOULD YOUR
DINOSAUR'S EVIL
TWIN LOOK LIKE?

HELPFUL HACKS

As you work, you might discover ways to make challenging tasks easier. Try these simple tricks and **techniques** as you construct your dinosaur!

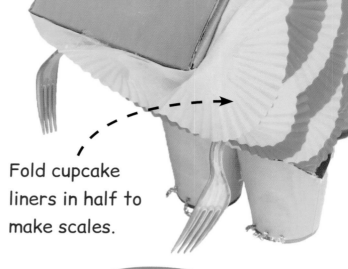

Fold cupcake liners in half to make scales.

Using Velcro allows you to change the position of your dino's head.

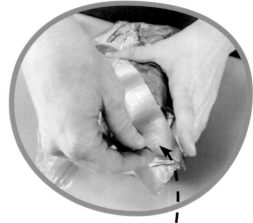

Put crumpled newspaper in a plastic bag. Then wrap the bag in duct tape, forming as you go to make any shape you want.

PROBLEM—SOLVE!
See page 26

Bend paper clips into shapes and cover them with duct tape.

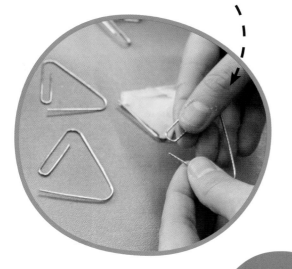

Cut a notch to make shapes fit together perfectly.

Use a soda bottle top with caps glued together for a removable neck.

Brass fasteners allow the mouth to open and close.

⚠ STUCK?

MAKERS AROUND THE WORLD SHARE THEIR PROJECTS ON THE INTERNET AND IN BOOKS. IF YOU HAVE A MAKERSPACE PROBLEM, THERE'S A GOOD CHANCE SOMEONE ELSE HAS ALREADY FOUND A SOLUTION. SEARCH THE INTERNET OR LIBRARY FOR HELPFUL ADVICE AS YOU MAKE YOUR PROJECTS!

GET INSPIRED

Get inspiration from the real world before you start building your dinosaur!

LOOK AT DINOSAURS

Look at images and models of real dinosaurs. They came in all shapes and sizes. They also had many different features, such as claws, teeth, and spikes. How can you combine these features in your dino?

LOOK AT STRUCTURES

Think about human-made structures that share your dinosaur's shape. A stegosaurus has a similar shape to a coffee table. A *Tyrannosaurus rex* is shaped a bit like a tower. What structures look like your dinosaur?

LOOK AT NATURE

Nature is full of amazing shapes and patterns. These can give you ideas for your dino's **details**. Look at fish scales, tree bark, shark teeth, and more to get ideas for your dinosaur!

PROBLEM-SOLVE

No makerspace project goes exactly as planned. But with a little creativity, you can find a **solution** to any problem.

FIGURE OUT THE PROBLEM

Maybe your standing dino tips over. Why do you think this is happening? Thinking about what may be causing the problem can lead you to a solution!

SOLUTION:
Anchor the tail with poster putty.

SOLUTION:
Spread the feet for a wider base.

BRAINSTORM AND TEST

Try coming up with three possible **solutions** to any problem.
Maybe your dino's head falls off the body. You could:

1. Make the head out of lighter materials.

2. Use a super-sticky connecting material to attach the head.

3. Change the head's position on the body.

Test all three and see which works best!

ADAPT

Still stuck? Try a different material or change the **technique** slightly.

COLLABORATE

Collaboration means working together with others. There are tons of ways to collaborate to build a dinosaur!

ASK A FELLOW MAKER

Talk to a friend, classmate, or family member. Other makers can help you think through the different steps to building a dinosaur. These helpers can also lend a pair of hands during construction!

ASK AN ADULT HELPER

This could be a teacher, librarian, grandparent, or any trusted adult. Describe what you want a material to do instead of asking for a specific material. Your helper might think of items you didn't know existed!

ASK AN EXPERT

A building **expert**, such as an engineer, could tell you how to build a sturdy structure. A dinosaur expert could help you understand how real dinosaurs looked and behaved!

THE WORLD IS A MAKERSPACE!

Your dino may look finished, but don't close your makerspace toolbox yet. Think about what would make your dinosaur better. What would you do differently if you built it again? What would happen if you used different **techniques** or materials?

DON'T STOP AT DINOSAURS

You can use your makerspace toolbox beyond the makerspace! You might use it to accomplish everyday tasks, such as math homework or cleaning your room. But makers use the same toolbox to do big things. One day, these tools could help cure illnesses or clean our air and water. Turn your world into a makerspace! What problems could you solve?

GLOSSARY

buoyant (BOY-uhnt) – capable of floating.

collaborate – to work with others.

detail – a small part of something.

DNA – a material in the body that helps determine what features a living thing will inherit. "DNA" stands for deoxyribonucleic acid.

expert – a person who is very knowledgeable about a certain subject.

paleontologist (pay-lee-ahn-TAH-luh-jihst) – a person who studies fossils and ancient animals and plants.

permanent – meant to last for a very long time.

solution – an answer to, or a way to solve, a problem.

technique – a method or style in which something is done.

waterproof – made so that water can't get in.

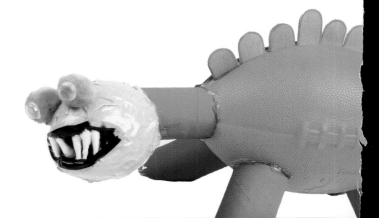